D0398101

YOU'RE NOT OLD YOU'RE *Vintage*

summersdale

YOU'RE NOT OLD, YOU'RE VINTAGE

First published in 2014

This edition copyright © Summersdale Publishers Ltd, 2017

Research by Sarah Viner

Summersdale Publishers Ltd
46 West Street
Chichester
West Sussex
PO19 1RP
UK

www.summersdale.com

Printed and bound in Croatia

ISBN: 978-1-78685-012-6

Substantial discounts on bulk quantities of Summersdale books are available to corporations, professional associations and other organisations. For details contact general enquiries: telephone: +44 (0) 1243 771107, fax: +44 (0) 1243 786300 or email: enquiries@summersdale.com.

Laughter is timeless.
Imagination has no age.
And dreams are forever.

WALT DISNEY

YOU CAN'T TURN
BACK THE CLOCK.
BUT YOU CAN WIND
IT UP AGAIN.

BONNIE PRUDDEN

Eventually you will reach
a point when you stop
lying about your age
and start bragging
about it.

WILL ROGERS

With mirth and laughter let old wrinkles come.

WILLIAM SHAKESPEARE

You don't get older, you get better.

SHIRLEY BASSEY

TO ....

FROM ....

Grow old along with me!
The best is yet to be.

ROBERT BROWNING

THE GOOD OLD DAYS ARE NOW.

TOM CLANCY

The three ages of man:
youth, middle age,
and 'my word you
do look well'.

JUNE WHITFIELD

Nice to be here?
At my age it's nice
to be anywhere.

GEORGE BURNS

I will never give in to old age until I become old. And I'm not old yet!

TINA TURNER

A diplomat is a man
who always remembers
a woman's birthday but
never remembers her age.

ROBERT FROST

AGE IS AN ISSUE OF
MIND OVER MATTER.
IF YOU DON'T MIND,
IT DOESN'T MATTER.

MARK TWAIN

If wrinkles must be written upon our brows, let them not be written upon the heart.

The best time to plant a tree was 20 years ago. The second best time is now.

CHINESE PROVERB

THE YEARS TEACH MUCH WHICH THE DAYS NEVER KNOW.

RALPH WALDO EMERSON

The old age of an eagle
is better than the youth
of a sparrow.

PROVERB

I want to live to
be 120. That's when
I will start worrying
about my age.

HELENA CHRISTENSEN

The young sow wild oats. The old grow sage.

WINSTON CHURCHILL

Whenever the talk
turns to age, I say
I am 49 plus VAT.

LIONEL BLAIR

ONE SHOULD NEVER
TRUST A WOMAN
WHO TELLS HER REAL
AGE. IF SHE TELLS
THAT, SHE'LL TELL
ANYTHING.

OSCAR WILDE

The first sign of maturity
is the discovery that
the volume knob also
turns to the left.

JERRY M. WRIGHT

Growing old is
compulsory. Growing
up is optional.

BOB MONKHOUSE

IT'S IMPORTANT TO HAVE A TWINKLE IN YOUR WRINKLE.

ANONYMOUS

I don't want to retire.
I'm not that good at
crossword puzzles.

NORMAN MAILER

We are always the
same age inside.

GERTRUDE STEIN

The secret to staying
young is to live honestly,
eat slowly and lie
about your age.

LUCILLE BALL

One of the good things about getting older is you find you're more interesting than most of the people you meet.

LEE MARVIN

I LOVE EVERYTHING THAT'S OLD: OLD FRIENDS, OLD TIMES, OLD MANNERS, OLD BOOKS, OLD WINE.

OLIVER GOLDSMITH

Youth has no age.

PABLO PICASSO

To me, old age is
always 15 years
older than I am.

BERNARD BARUCH

OLD AGE IS LIKE
EVERYTHING ELSE.
TO MAKE A SUCCESS
OF IT, YOU'VE GOT TO
START YOUNG.

THEODORE ROOSEVELT

Life is either a daring adventure or nothing.

HELEN KELLER

I don't feel old. I don't feel anything till noon. That's when it's time for my nap.

BOB HOPE

I used to think I'd like less grey hair. Now I'd like more of it.

RICHIE BENAUD

The man of
wisdom is the
man of years.

EDWARD YOUNG

YOUTH DISSERVES; MIDDLE AGE CONSERVES; OLD AGE PRESERVES.

MARTIN H. FISCHER

At my age 'getting lucky'
means finding my car in
the parking lot.

ANONYMOUS

I'll keep swivelling my hips until they need replacing.

TOM JONES

AS YOU GET OLDER,
THE PICKINGS GET
SLIMMER, BUT THE
PEOPLE DON'T.

CARRIE FISHER

The easiest way to
diminish the appearance
of wrinkles is to keep
your glasses off when
you look in the mirror.

JOAN RIVERS

One of the best parts
of growing older?
You can flirt all you
like since you've
become harmless.

LIZ SMITH

Being 80 makes me
feel like an authority,
especially when I say,
'I don't know.'

PETER USTINOV

Just remember, when you're over the hill, you begin to pick up speed.

CHARLES M. SCHULZ

OLD MEN ARE FOND
OF GIVING GOOD
ADVICE, TO CONSOLE
THEMSELVES FOR
BEING NO LONGER IN
A POSITION TO GIVE
BAD EXAMPLES.

FRANÇOIS DE LA ROCHEFOUCAULD

I'm not sure that old age isn't the best part of life.

C. S. LEWIS

The whiter my hair
becomes, the more ready
people are to believe
what I say.

BERTRAND RUSSELL

AS WE GROW OLDER,
OUR BODIES GET
SHORTER AND OUR
ANECDOTES LONGER.

ROBERT QUILLEN

Life is a great big canvas,
and you should throw all
the paint on it you can.

DANNY KAYE

When grace is joined
with wrinkles, it is
adorable. There is an
unspeakable dawn in
happy old age.

VICTOR HUGO

I absolutely refuse
to reveal my age.
What am I – a car?

CYNDI LAUPER

A prune is an experienced plum.

JOHN H. TRATTNER

SOME PEOPLE REACH THE AGE OF 60 BEFORE OTHERS.

SAMUEL HOOD

You can only be
young once, but
you can always
be immature.

DAVE BARRY

Birthdays are good for you. Statistics show that the people who have the most live the longest.

LARRY LORENZONI

THERE'S ONE ADVANTAGE TO BEING 102. THERE'S NO PEER PRESSURE.

DENNIS WOLFBERG

Age merely shows
what children
we remain.

JOHANN WOLFGANG VON GOETHE

Time and trouble will
tame an advanced
young woman, but an
advanced old woman is
uncontrollable by any
earthly force.

DOROTHY L. SAYERS

The ageing process has you firmly in its grasp if you never get the urge to throw a snowball.

DOUG LARSON

Seize the moment.
Remember all
those women on
the *Titanic* who
waved off the
dessert cart.

ERMA BOMBECK

I'M AIMING BY
THE TIME I'M 50
TO STOP BEING
AN ADOLESCENT.

WENDY COPE

I don't know how I got
over the hill without
getting to the top.

WILL ROGERS

Age isn't how old you are but how old you feel.

GABRIEL GARCÍA MÁRQUEZ

A BIRTHDAY IS JUST THE FIRST DAY OF ANOTHER 365-DAY JOURNEY AROUND THE SUN. ENJOY THE TRIP.

ANONYMOUS

We don't stop playing
because we grow old;
we grow old because
we stop playing.

GEORGE BERNARD SHAW

If I had my life to live over again, I'd make the same mistakes, only sooner.

TALLULAH BANKHEAD

When I was a boy
the Dead Sea was
only sick.

GEORGE BURNS

Cherish all your happy
moments; they make
a fine cushion for
old age.

CHRISTOPHER MORLEY

YOUTH IS THE TIME
FOR ADVENTURES OF
THE BODY, BUT AGE
FOR THE TRIUMPHS
OF THE MIND.

LOGAN PEARSALL SMITH

Allow me to put the
record straight. I am 46
and have been for some
years past.

ERICA JONG

Everyone is the age of their heart.

GUATEMALAN PROVERB

EVERYTHING SLOWS
DOWN WITH AGE,
EXCEPT THE TIME IT
TAKES CAKE AND ICE
CREAM TO REACH
YOUR HIPS.

JOHN WAGNER

I intend to
live forever,
or die trying.

GROUCHO MARX

Each year it grows harder
to make ends meet –
the ends I refer to are
hands and feet.

RICHARD ARMOUR

My grandmother is over 80 and still doesn't need glasses. Drinks right out of the bottle.

HENNY YOUNGMAN

Another belief of mine:
that everyone else my
age is an adult, whereas I
am merely in disguise.

MARGARET ATWOOD

I'M HAPPY TO REPORT
THAT MY INNER CHILD
IS STILL AGELESS.

JAMES BROUGHTON

Age does not
diminish the extreme
disappointment of
having a scoop of
ice cream fall
from the cone.

JIM FIEBIG

White hair often
covers the head, but
the heart that holds
it is ever young.

HONORÉ DE BALZAC

I DON'T BELIEVE IN AGEING. I BELIEVE IN FOREVER ALTERING ONE'S ASPECT TO THE SUN.

VIRGINIA WOOLF

Age seldom arrives
smoothly or quickly.
It's more often a
succession of jerks.

JEAN RHYS

The best mirror is an old friend.

GEORGE HERBERT

Age is just a number.
It's totally irrelevant
unless, of course, you
happen to be a bottle
of wine.

JOAN COLLINS

You're getting old when
the only thing you want
for your birthday is not
to be reminded of it.

ANONYMOUS

THE OLDER YOU GET, THE BETTER YOU USED TO BE.

JOHN McENROE

My husband's idea of
a good night out is a
good night in.

MAUREEN LIPMAN

If I could get back my youth I'd do anything in the world, except get up early, take exercise or be respectable.

OSCAR WILDE

I BELIEVE IN LOYALTY.
WHEN A WOMAN
REACHES A CERTAIN
AGE SHE LIKES,
SHE SHOULD
STICK WITH IT.

EVA GABOR

Old age and treachery
will always beat youth
and exuberance.

DAVID MAMET

The key to successful
ageing is to pay as
little attention to
it as possible.

JUDITH REGAN

I plan on growing old
much later in life, or
maybe not at all.

PATTY CAREY

I'm too old to do
things by half.

LOU REED

FUN IS LIKE
LIFE INSURANCE;
THE OLDER YOU GET,
THE MORE IT COSTS.

KIN HUBBARD

I can still enjoy sex
at 74. I live at 75,
so it's no distance.

BOB MONKHOUSE

In youth we run into difficulties. In old age difficulties run into us.

BEVERLY SILLS

TO STOP AGEING —
KEEP ON RAGING.

MICHAEL FORBES

We turn not older
with years, but
newer every day.

EMILY DICKINSON

All would live long,
but none would
be old.

BENJAMIN FRANKLIN

Age is only
a number.

ANONYMOUS

Anyone who keeps the
ability to see beauty
never grows old.

FRANZ KAFKA

OLD AGE IS AN EXCELLENT TIME FOR OUTRAGE. MY GOAL IS TO SAY OR DO AT LEAST ONE OUTRAGEOUS THING EVERY WEEK.

LOUIS KRONENBERGER

I must be getting old.
I can't take yes for
an answer.

FRED ALLEN

When it comes
to staying young,
a mindlift beats
a facelift any day.

MARTY BUCELLA

IF YOU WANT A THING WELL DONE, GET A COUPLE OF OLD BROADS TO DO IT.

BETTE DAVIS

Growing old is no more
than a bad habit which
a busy man has no
time to form.

ANDRÉ MAUROIS

As you get older three
things happen. The first
is your memory goes...
and I can't remember
the other two.

NORMAN WISDOM

Autumn is the mellower season, and what we lose in flowers, we more than gain in fruits.

SAMUEL BUTLER

It takes a long time
to become young.

PABLO PICASSO

OLD AGE ISN'T SO BAD WHEN YOU CONSIDER THE ALTERNATIVE.

MAURICE CHEVALIER

If you rest,
you rust.

HELEN HAYES

You are never too old to
set another goal or to
dream a new dream.

LES BROWN

LAUGHTER DOESN'T REQUIRE TEETH.

BILL NEWTON

Men are like wine –
some turn to vinegar,
but the best improve
with age.

C. E. M. JOAD

Growing old is not growing up.

DOUGLAS HORTON

Live your life
and forget
your age.

NORMAN VINCENT PEALE

Old age is like a plane
flying through a storm.
Once you are aboard
there is nothing you
can do.

GOLDA MEIR

SOME DAY YOU WILL
BE OLD ENOUGH TO
START READING FAIRY
TALES AGAIN.

C. S. LEWIS

The older one grows,
the more one
likes indecency.

VIRGINIA WOOLF

Alas, after a certain
age every man is
responsible for
his face.

ALBERT CAMUS

I DON'T PLAN
TO GROW OLD
GRACEFULLY.
I PLAN TO HAVE
FACELIFTS UNTIL
MY EARS MEET.

RITA RUDNER

You know you're
getting old when
the candles cost
more than the cake.

BOB HOPE

Older people
shouldn't eat health
food, they need all the
preservatives they
can get.

ROBERT ORBEN

I'm 60 years of age.
That's 16 Celsius!

GEORGE CARLIN

You can't help getting older, but you don't have to get old.

GEORGE BURNS

YOUTH IS THE GIFT OF NATURE, BUT AGE IS A WORK OF ART.

GARSON KANIN

Even if there's snow on
the roof, it doesn't mean
the fire has gone out in
the furnace.

ANONYMOUS

I'm like old wine.
They don't bring me
out very often, but
I'm well preserved.

ROSE KENNEDY

I DON'T NEED YOU TO REMIND ME OF MY AGE. I HAVE A BLADDER TO DO THAT FOR ME.

STEPHEN FRY

Men chase golf balls
when they're too old to
chase anything else.

GROUCHO MARX

The older I get, the older old is.

TOM BAKER

Forty is the old age of
youth; fifty the youth
of old age.

VICTOR HUGO

You only live once,
but if you do it right,
once is enough.

MAE WEST

INSIDE EVERY OLD
PERSON IS A YOUNG
PERSON WONDERING
WHAT HAPPENED.

ANONYMOUS

Nobody loves life
like him that's
growing old.

SOPHOCLES

The longer I live the more beautiful life becomes.

FRANK LLOYD WRIGHT

WISDOM DOESN'T
NECESSARILY
COME WITH AGE.
SOMETIMES AGE
JUST SHOWS UP
ALL BY ITSELF.

TOM WILSON

The best tunes are played on the oldest fiddles.

RALPH WALDO EMERSON

Do not worry about avoiding temptation. As you grow older it will avoid you.

JOEY ADAMS

The old believe everything,
the middle-aged suspect
everything, the young
know everything.

OSCAR WILDE

I'm like a good cheese.
I'm just getting mouldy
enough to be interesting.

PAUL NEWMAN

I ADVISE YOU TO GO
ON LIVING SOLELY TO
ENRAGE THOSE WHO
ARE PAYING YOUR
ANNUITIES. IT IS THE
ONLY PLEASURE I
HAVE LEFT.

VOLTAIRE

Youth is a wonderful
thing. What a crime to
waste it on children.

GEORGE BERNARD SHAW

I refuse to admit I'm more than 52, even if that does make my sons illegitimate.

NANCY ASTOR

LIVE EACH DAY AS IF YOUR LIFE HAD JUST BEGUN.

JOHANN WOLFGANG VON GOETHE

Laugh like you're 10,
party like you're 20,
travel like you're 30,
think like you're 40,
advise like you're 50,
care like you're 60,
love like you're 70.

ANONYMOUS

Don't let ageing get
you down. It's too
hard to get back up.

JOHN WAGNER

I'm at an age when
my back goes out
more than I do.

PHYLLIS DILLER

Looking 50 is great
– if you're 60.

JOAN RIVERS

FOR ALL THE
ADVANCES IN
MEDICINE, THERE
IS STILL NO CURE
FOR THE COMMON
BIRTHDAY.

JOHN GLENN

Wrinkles should merely
indicate where the
smiles have been.

MARK TWAIN

Youth would be an ideal
state if it came a little
later in life.

HERBERT HENRY ASQUITH

TIME IS A DRESSMAKER SPECIALISING IN ALTERATIONS.

FAITH BALDWIN

Old age: the crown
of life, our play's
last act.

CICERO

I still have a full deck; I just shuffle slower now.

ANONYMOUS

Old age is no place for sissies.

BETTE DAVIS

No man is ever old enough to know better.

HOLBROOK JACKSON

THE GOLDEN AGE
IS BEFORE US, NOT
BEHIND US.

WILLIAM SHAKESPEARE

If you're interested in finding out more about our books, find us on Facebook at Summersdale Publishers and follow us on Twitter at @Summersdale.

www.summersdale.com